SHOW ME THE PLAN

HOW TO MAKE MONEY KNOWING THE PLAN

JEFF NKELE MBAI

SHOW ME THE PLAN!

"Dissecting the Plan Networking System To <u>Maximize</u> Profits & Even Start Your Own Company!"

Copyright © 2018 by Jeff NkeleMbai

All rights reserved. No part of this teaching material should be reproduced or transmitted by any means or in any form, including recording, photocopying, or other mechanical or electronic means without the expressed written permission of the author or the publisher except if it is quoted for noncommercial or critical reviews.

For permission request, direct your request to the address below:

Gtext Group,

51/52, Ijaye Road,

Ogba, Lagos,

Nigeria, Africa.

Disclaimer

This book is not designed to be used as a source of business, legal, financial, or accounting advice. Readers are advised to consult competent professionals if they need business, legal, financial, or accounting advice.

While we have made reasonable attempts to guarantee the accuracy of the content of this publication, the author cannot be held responsible for omissions, errors, or contrary interpretation of the content as well as cost or damages incurred through such omission or interpretation.

While some previous examples of results of some actions are used occasionally in this publication, the examples are nothing but what they are. They are not used as the model that the reader must stick to.

The author's personal experience forms the foundation of this book. Thus, he's not responsible for whatever you do with any information contained in the book. Use your discretion to choose any information that suits you and use it without passing any liability or responsibility to the author.

Any resemblance to people, alive or dead, fictitious or real, is accidental. There is no deliberate slight on organizations or people if such seems to be implied in the book.

You can download the book or print it out for reading. However, you are using the information contained in the book at your own risk.

CHAPTER ONE

Those Who Fail to Plan, Plan to Fail

Welcome to Show Me the Plan – Part 1. This book is the first in a 2-part series that promises to be both exciting and informative.

Why did I take the pain to write this informative book? If you are conversant with the network marketing industry, you won't be surprised at the rate at which the higher number of new distributors invests their time and resources in network marketing training. This is because the majority of such network marketers have little or no idea of the principle behind the compensation plan offered by their company.

On a yearly basis, networking marketing teams and companies around the world spend thousands of dollars on training employees and marketers on their plans. This is a necessity in view of many people's attitude towards marketing plans. They find it too confusing while some people don't attach much seriousness to the concept, denying themselves the opportunity to be informed and well-equipped about it.

Isn't this disturbing? Well, consider these:

- Would you pursue a profession if your career path is not well defined?
- Would you take up a job if you have no idea about your salary/wage?
- Would you consider doing a money give away?

The answers to these questions are pretty obvious. However, in network marketing, a comprehensive understanding of the existing marketing plan, both that of your company and other companies in the industry, will prove invaluable to your success. Such knowledge won't only save you time but will play a crucial role in influencing your network marketing career. Those who are planning to launch an online or offline network marketing company will need this information and knowledge more than others.

When I first joined the network marketing business, I had no clue about what my company's plan was. When potential prospects inquired about my income at the level, I couldn't give a straight answer without calling my upline to get the answer. I did that in the presence of the prospects. That's laughable. When the prospecting session was over, I had called my upline several times. I was fortunate that the prospect did sign up regardless of my performance.

Some people are not that fortunate and have lost thousands of dollars to lack of understanding of the plan and poor planning. Note that understanding such plans is not rocket science. With some mechanics and a simple calculation, you can master the principle.

When you are through with this book, you would have learnt how to:
- Understand the different typical plans and how to monetize them.
- Use the knowledge of companies' plans to make the right choice with respect to a network marketing company.
- Develop self-confidence while dealing with prospects.
- Winning other networkers to your company by highlighting the superiority of your plan to theirs.
- Develop an effective strategy that can assist you to build a durable network with long-term goals.
- Avoid some costly mistakes that may undermine your success by getting the right people for your new downlines with a view to getting the best for them and maximizing your profits.

- Launch a new network marketing company of your own in the best way that will save you from potential problems and disaster.

What are the best ways to achieve this? This and other questions will be answered in the next chapter.

CHAPTER TWO

Terminology and Jargon You Can't Live Without

If you are contemplating starting your own company, it is advisable that you familiarize yourself with the basic terminologies that are used in the industry. Some of these terminologies are discussed below:

1. **Builder**

This term refers to a distributor that is working round the clock to get downlines. Note that a builder is quite different from a customer who recommends a product to his or her friends after consuming them.

2. **Upline**

An upline is someone above you in the company's hierarchy. Depending on when you join a company and the number of people above your upline, you may have more than an upline, possibly as much as 10 or above.

Your upline is responsible for your affairs and success in the company.

3. **Upline leader/mentor**

An upline mentor or leader is an upline that you have taken as your mentor in the business. He or she is your reference whenever you need some practical advice and tips on the best way to build your business.

Such an upline has the responsibility of assisting you to be successful in the network marketing business.

4. **Sponsor**

This is the person who is directly above you in the company; perhaps, the person brought you into the company.

5. **Downline**

The downline is someone below you in the organization. You are entitled to some commissions from your downlines, although the commission is a factor of the company as well as the deeper the downlines are in the organization.

Sometimes, you may not know your downline personally if he or she is very far below you in the hierarchy.

6. Sideline/crossline

You don't share the same company with these people. You equally have no financial relationship with them as well. However, these people may be considered as your valuable allies or worst competitors, depending on your company's principle.

Note that these people are also members of your upline's immediate group. Thus, when you help the sidelines, you are invariably assisting your upline and the members of his or her group.

7. Frontline

The frontlines are downlines that you personally sponsor or you are directly above them. Since you brought them into the company, their success is your personal responsibility. How you handle your frontline is a crucial factor that will determine the failure or success of your downline group, excluding no one.

8. Leg

A member of your network, beginning from someone you personally sponsor is a leg. This person and other members of your downline are jointly seen as one of your numerous legs. As a distributor, you can develop several legs simultaneously.

9. Width

The level of the downline of your downline is referred to as depth. To build a secure organization, you must build a good depth first.

10. Override

An override simply implies that you get some commissions from your downline's group. This is usually calculated on only your frontline.

11. Profit sharing pool

This is a special bonus that is paid to some achievers who have excelled in the business after reaching some conditions set in the company's marketing plan. The total collection of sales registered by all the distributors of a company makes up the pool. This is regardless of whether your sideline contributes to the sales volume or not.

12. Maintenance

The maintenance is the mandatory sales volume that is expected of a distributor. Sometimes, though, it may be optional if some criteria are brought into the equation. The objective of the maintenance is to override all your downlines and make you eligible to share profit with the company. It also serves the purpose of maintaining your distributorship status or some rank. The company enforces maintenance since it isn't a charity but a money-making business.

13. Total Payout

The payout is the percentage set aside from sales as an incentive for the distributors while the company keeps whatever remains after that.

CHAPTER THREE

Removing common misconceptions

There are many misconceptions in digital marketing, especially with regards to their compensation plan.

It is obvious that the compensation plan is nothing but a side offer and not that important. The most important thing is to recruit distributors. A plan will either have a positive or a negative impact on a company. Attrition is usually caused by the need for distributors to survive in the business. On a personal note, will you feel comfortable with the business if it is not financially rewarding?

Some factors such as maintenance, payout, and joining fee are very important to this business. If a business can boast of impressively high maintenance but that is not reflected in sales, the business will soon be out of business.

It is natural that builders will take their jobs seriously if they are guaranteed the best compensation plan. Some people have a lukewarm attitude towards their business and unfortunately, pass the buck to the plan when they fail.

They sometimes blame the management as well, referring to them as a scam. If you have to move on to another business, ensure that you don't use your exit to justify your failure, rather, have a legit business reason for doing that.

I do take the time to give a comprehensive explanation of the plan to my prospects to ensure that they understand it better.

A new person may reject your offer if he or she is confused while explaining the new plan to him or her.

You must endeavour to keep the plan explanation very simple. Rather than focus on explaining the features, focus on the benefits.

If you must start a network marketing company, it is advisable that you outline the benefits of the company with regards to the potential earnings and spare people the need for stressful thinking.

If I must start a new marketing company, a good plan is all that I need.

A network marketing company's success will be determined by a lot of factors. The manager is one of the most important factors to be considered. Without a solid and credible management team, a seemingly successful company will fold up. Other factors include the product. A viable product will guarantee repeat sales and cash flow for the entire distributors and the company as well. The company's plan should align with other factors.

If the payout is good, there will be a massive joining of the company

If the distributors are offered good commission, the product must be carefully inspected. If the mark-up is on the high side, it may offer the best short-term benefit for the distributors. In the long run, however, the consumers will be negatively affected. That may end up devaluing the product.

Good mark-up and repeat sales are two factors that a product depends on. Otherwise, the company won't pass the test of time. Most companies have the attitude of grabbing a product and assign a good mark-up to it in order to attract builders without giving a second thought to its survivability.

Recognizing the plan mechanics

Now that marketing plan's importance has been highlighted, it is imperative that its basic mechanics are well understood as well. This concept will be treated gradually.

The outline will be discussed under these topics:

1. What are the best strategies for building downline?
2. How does the strategy align with the product?
3. If I float a company with the feature, what are the potential weaknesses and strengths?

CHAPTER FOUR

Point Value to Cash Calculation

In network marketing, the point value is sometimes defined the monetary value you get from purchasing a product. Let's consider this illustration:

Scenario 1:

Let's say, a product costs $100 and each dollar spent on the product gives you 1 PV: I get paid on 100 PV for purchasing $100 worth of products and if I am eligible for 10% override, **I earn $10**

Hence the dollar to PV ratio is $1:1 PV – a dollar to dollar equal comparison

SCENARIO 2

Sometimes, the same price of a product will only give you 0.5 PV for each $1 spent. I get paid on 50PV for purchasing $100 in this scenario. If I am eligible for 10% override, **I earn only $5**

Hence the dollar to PV ratio now is $2:1 PV – you don't get as much as 1:1because you have to spend more to earn more points

SCENARIO 3

Certain companies might give away promotions for products and offer **$1:1.1 PV** so if you **buy $100, you get paid on $110** value. At 10%, **I earn $11 – more commission from the company on the product for less spent buying it,**

Downline Building Strategies

If I must generate huge volume for my downline group, I will implore them to be more focused on selling more of the products with a high point value. This ensures that they earn more while spending less.

Product synergy

Products that are promoted offer higher PV ratio than others. Outsourced products from outside companies offer smaller PV, but in some cases, may offer the same PV as promoted products. Since they have to pay the outsourced company, the business volume may be smaller.
This type of products offer lower pay but offers distributors a good variety.

Starting a new company

When distributors are offered good PV to dollar ratio, they are encouraged since that translates to more payment without putting in more effort. If I must move high-ticket items such as air treatment systems, water filter, or expensive cookware. In order to sell these items fast, I will offer the distributors high PV incentive and make good money from it.

CHAPTER FIVE

Payout Transparency

A company must have a transparent marketing plan and must be written in simple terms that all and sundry can easily understand. The payout transparency is a reference to the money set aside to be paid to the listed distributors.

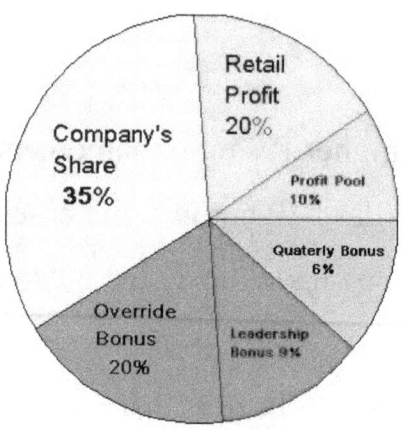

Downline Building Strategies

The transparent payout is a very useful tool for motivating your downline. This is particularly true for new prospects who are still trying to evaluate the company. When you teach them the meaning of the percentages, they will be more equipped to make more sales.

Product synergy

Product synergy is also important because when the mark-up is too high, retail customers may find the product affordability very difficult. It is customary in multi-level marketing to pay distributors across many levels. Thus, if a product can be sold without bringing people in to join the company, the product obviously enjoys a strong demand.

Starting a new company

Before you start a company, make an advanced calculation of the payout and make a decision about the mark-up as well. When handling the Binary Plans, you must be extremely careful. This is important if you want to prevent overpaying your distributors, lest your company goes bankrupt.

CHAPTER SIX

Buy Back Policy

The buy back policy is crucial to the company's success. It entails the terms and conditions that serve as protection for distributors in the event that they quit the business and demand their money. This is more practical for offline companies. Successful and strong companies usually put in place a good money-back guarantee that covers the product in case of partial or full usage. The guarantee makes it mandatory for the company to absorb any risk associated with the product because you can't rule out the possibility of some people quitting the network marketing. There are individuals who are also out to play games with the company and want to try the product freely.

In some countries, a 10-day cooling off period is usually offered. Sometimes, this may be up to 6 or 12 months during which a 90-100% refund may be made on the product irrespective of whether the product is unused or used during the period. This is due to the existing laws put in place by the Federal Trade Commission or the country in question.

Downline building strategies

To prevent a buy-back policy from being implemented, an upline is forced to give his or her best. This is because activating this policy implies that the upline may lose future income or have his or her commission deducted or recalled. This is the normal procedure in network marketing. The upline has the responsibility of ensuring that the downline succeed by teaching the basic skills they need to succeed so that even if the downlines quit the business, their customers will still remain loyal to the company. That's a good preventive measure against buy backs.

Product synergy

In a direct product selling or network marketing, positive testimonials are a powerful driving force. When potential consumers are offered money back guaranteed, their confidence in the product increases.

Starting a new company

If you are contemplating starting a company, be careful if you wish to include the money back guarantee policy in your company. The guarantee implies that you are ready to absorb the costs of refunds. This is important because holding a customer's money back for whatever reason if a refund is made can destroy your company's reputation if they embark on negative word of mouth or report to consumers associations. Thus, it is imperative that you have a superb product to offer people; otherwise, your company will be accused of being a Pyramid or a Ponzi scheme.

CHAPTER SEVEN

Breakaway

Stairstep or Unilevel contains a concept that is known as a breakaway. This occurs when a downline outperforms his or her upline and reaches a target before the upline.

This is a typical example of breakaway:

Sponsor: 9% override

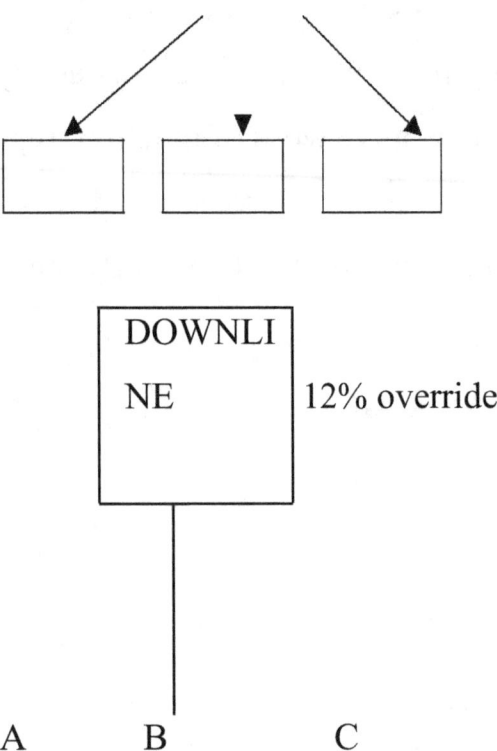

A   B   C

Let's assume that you must recruit downlines to the company if you wish to increase your commission to 12% from 9%. In this case, the SPONSOR must require that same number of downlines to be eligible for 12% commission but the downline reaches the target faster than the upline.

Network marketing is replete with such scenario because you don't have to slow down as a downline to give your upline a head start because people work differently.

The breakaway here implies that the upline won't enjoy receiving commissions from his group of downline forever, although this depends on the company's plan. The upline's commission will then be given to his or her upline. It is not unheard of for a downline to bypass his or her sponsor in which case the entire group will then join the new upline.

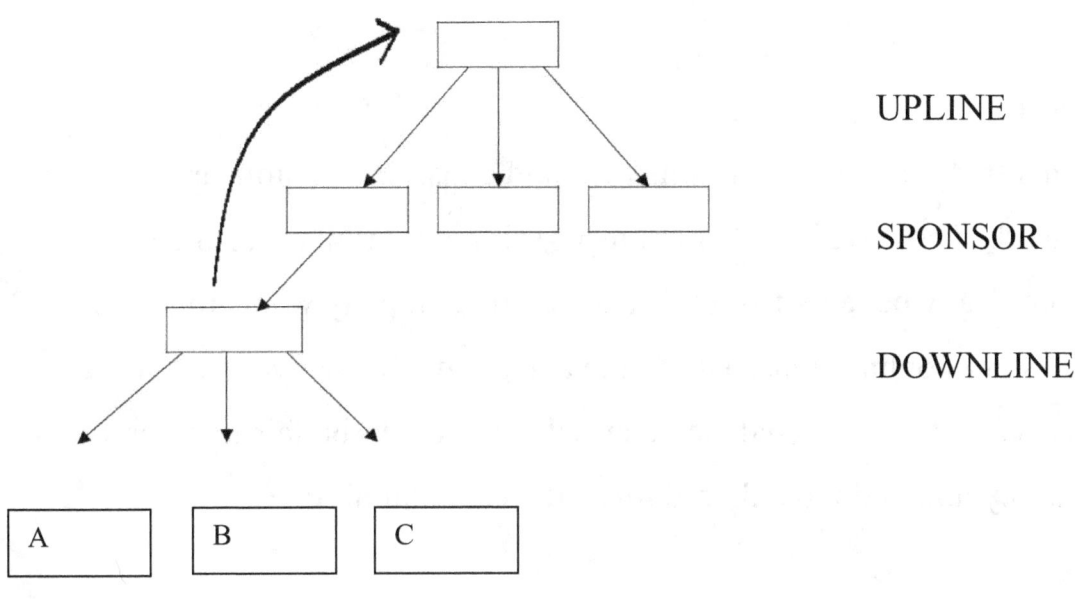

UPLINE

SPONSOR

DOWNLINE

Downline Building Strategies

Note that downlines and uplines work together with others to make a team that must work together. While assisting the downline, it is imperative that an upline doesn't leave his or her business unattended to. There are situations where a downline may decide to pause for the upline in order for both of them to work and achieve a common goal without leaving any member of the team behind.

Some issues such as sabotage where an upline deliberately slows his or her downline down as a preventive measure against breakaway can be effectively prevented if there is a good relationship and team planning.

Product Synergy

The disadvantages of breakaway notwithstanding, the upline mustn't relent in putting in the best effort into the business. For instance, if a downline grows very fast, the upline may be encouraged to work harder with a view to generating more sales that will attract more bonuses in addition to catching up with the high-flying downline.

Starting a New Company

Like every other thing, breakaway has its pros and cons. Distributors are rewarded for their hardwork. Those with more recruits or sell more products also get more rewards. The company benefits from this because no company wants to pay free loaders unnecessary commissions. The disadvantage of a breakaway is that the company must strive to strike a balance that will enable it to be fair to all parties. This is quite tricky and undoubtedly requires adequate planning.

CHAPTER EIGHT

Infinity Bonuses and Blocking

Once an achiever has succeeded in building a solid organization, he or she may get paid up to infinity commission levels by the company. This is great for distributors who aspire to take a leadership role and give their best to the company. Leaders who assist their downlines irrespective how low they are on the dowline ladder are also handsomely rewarded with infinity bonuses as well.

Check the diagram below:

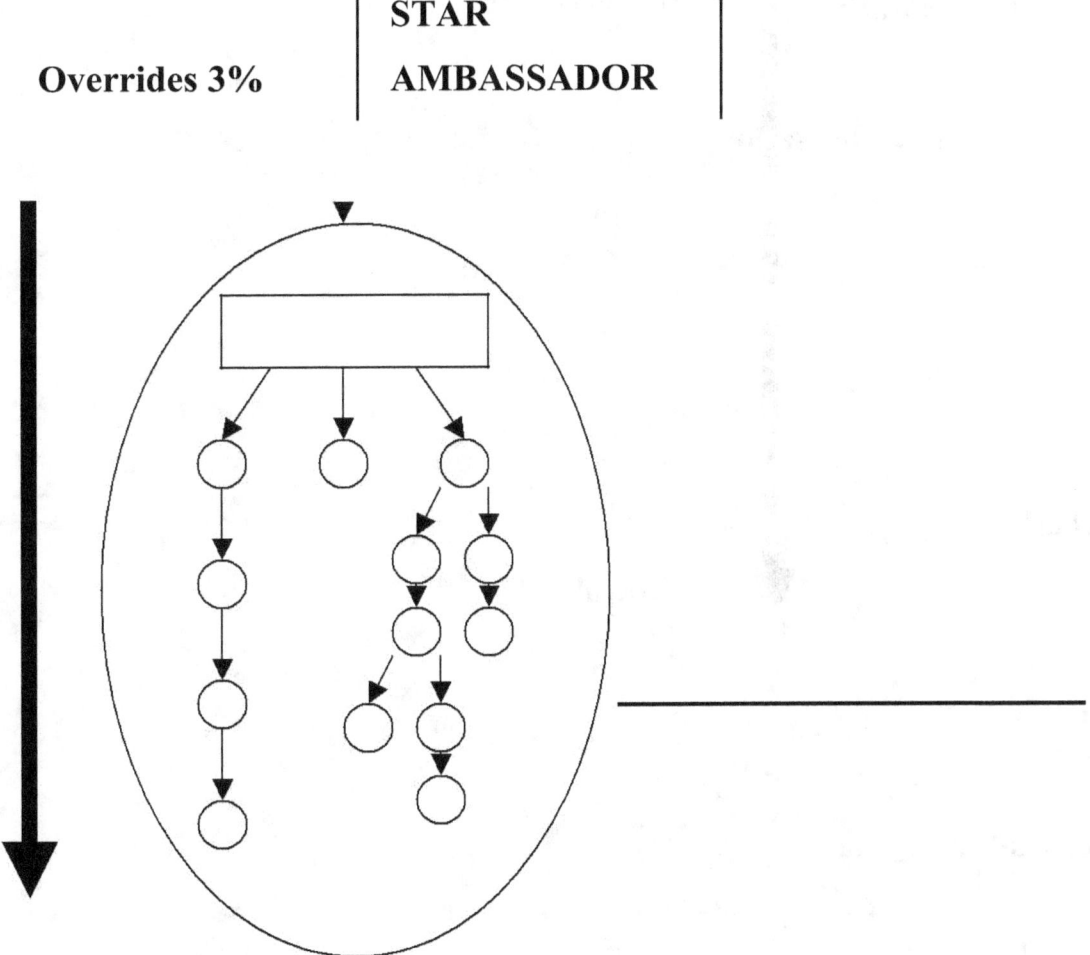

From the diagram, the star ambassador takes on the role of a leader who is providing the needed assistance to his or her downline group. For his or her efforts, the leader deserves a 3% commission from every member of the group.

If a downline can reach the same or higher level than the upline which we will refer to as the STAR AMBASSADOR here, the upline will be given infinity level that can override the downline up to one who is a Star Ambassador. This is another feature that is otherwise referred to as BLOCKING.

The next diagram explains the concept.

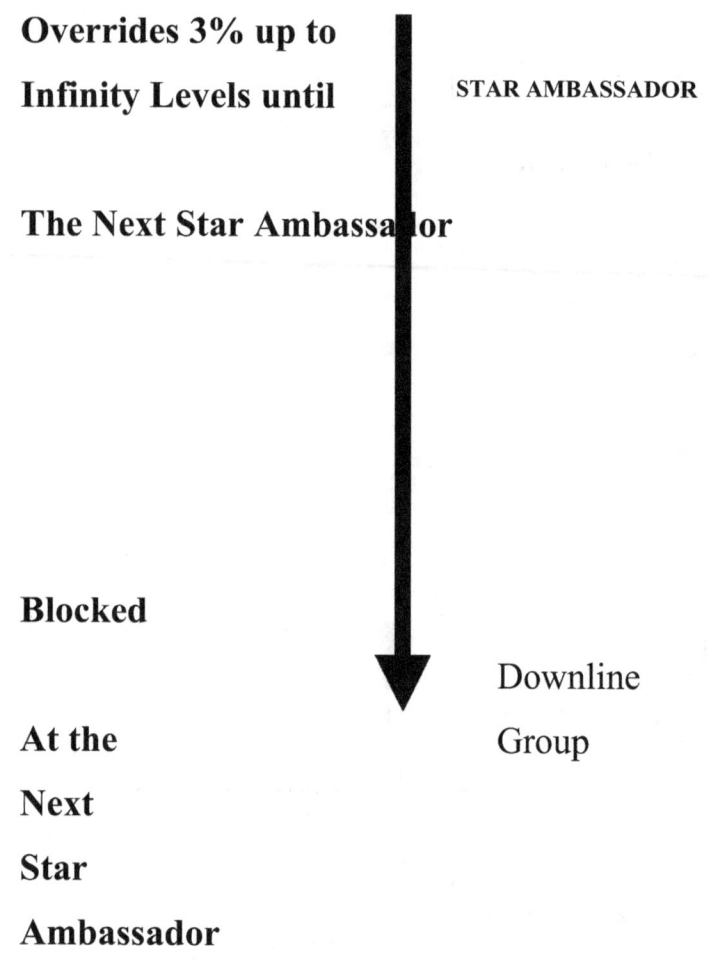

Overrides 3% up to Infinity Levels until

STAR AMBASSADOR

The Next Star Ambassador

Downline Group

Blocked

At the Next Star Ambassador

DOWNLINE

STAR

AMBASSADOR

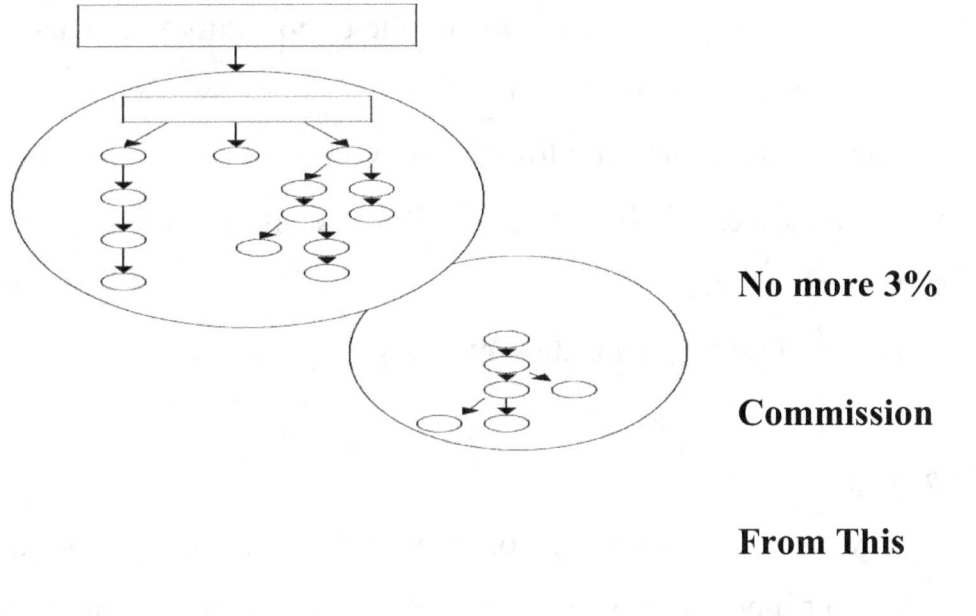

No more 3%

Commission

From This

Level Onwards

Note: For an upline's efforts to nurture a downline to strength, the company will award the upline with more bonuses. This may take the form of higher ranking or other bonuses.

Downline Building Strategies

You should endeavour to identify strong members of your downline and give them the right training that will prepare them for leadership roles and have something you can always leverage. This implies that a strong downline should be ready to receive the baton from you when you are not actively involved with the group. Although you are entitled to get infinity bonuses from your downline, the company will still reward you with a leadership bonus on the leader of the downline group. Note, however, that the leadership bonus is nothing compared to the retail bonus or override.

Product Synergy

If the infinity bonuses are done right, it may give you the opportunity to a massive and powerful source of residual income. If the members of your downline group are trained to use products without bias and loyally and you get 3% from all of them, your earnings will look like this if you have 1,000 downlines buying $500 worth of product each every month:

(3% * 1,000) * 500. This will give you $15,000 monthly.

Starting a New Company

If you want to start a new network marketing company and you intend giving out infinity bonuses, make your blocking system very clear. This is more important if overpaying forces you to use a binary plan.

This is a complex topic beyond the scope of this book. I will address that in the next book.

Summary

If you have gone this far, you have done a good job. Let me give you a quick summary of the important lessons in this book.

- The importance of marketing plan training.
- The terminology used in network marketing.
- Misconceptions about network marketing plan.
- How to build your downline with the right information.
- The importance of payout and PV to cash calculation.
- Breakaway, transparency, infinity bonuses, buy back policy, and blocking.

In the next book, the focus will be on the following:

- How to manipulate marketing plan mechanics to achieve much faster.
- Mastering the dreaded demotion.
- How to maximize your profits.
- How to leverage maintenance in any company.
-

Hope to see you at the top!

www.ingramcontent.com/pod-product-compliance
Lightning Source LLC
Chambersburg PA
CBHW081652220526
45468CB00009B/2626